BEACON SERMON OUTLINE SERIES

SERMON OUTLINES
FOR
Special
Occasions

GENE WILLIAMS

Beacon Hill Press of Kansas City
Kansas City, Missouri

Copyright 2003
by Beacon Hill Press of Kansas City

ISBN 083-412-0321

Printed in the
United States of America

Cover Design: Paul Franitza

Library of Congress Cataloging-in-Publication Data

Williams, Gene, 1932-
    Sermon outlines for special occasions / Gene Williams.
        p. cm. — (Beacon sermon outline series)
    ISBN 0-8341-2032-1 (pbk.)
    1. Sermons—Outlines, syllabi, etc. I. Title. II. Series.
    BV4223 .W4475 2003
    251'.02—dc21
                                                        2002151479

10   9   8   7   6   5   4   3   2   1

CONTENTS

PREFACE

Throughout the year there are special days that offer the opportunity for a pastor to emphasize different aspects of Christian living. The people who attend our churches are conscious of the fact that it is New Year's, Easter, Mother's Day, Father's Day, and other special days, and even funerals. We can minister to our people right where they are. Their minds are already on the subject because of the emphasis on that special day.

The pastor simply helps them to focus on the spiritual truths that apply to that specific interest.

Special day sermon outlines may, on occasions, interrupt other series. Even this interruption helps to spotlight the emphasis on the truth on those days.

The sermon outlines in this volume provide starting points from which one can make "special days" really special. Take these seeds, plant them in your fertile mind, water them with prayer, and see what God brings forth.

Sᴇʀᴍᴏɴ Oᴜᴛʟɪɴᴇꜱ ꜰᴏʀ ᴛʜᴇ Fɪʀꜱᴛ Sᴜɴᴅᴀʏ ᴏꜰ ᴛʜᴇ Nᴇᴡ Yᴇᴀʀ
A Yᴇᴀʀ ᴏꜰ Mᴀᴛᴜʀɪɴɢ

Hebrews 5

Introduction

A. There are several themes that could be our emphasis for this year. This could be a year of love, of obedience, of growing, or of faith.

B. We have chosen to make this a year of spiritual maturing.

C. Not every believer matures well. Some Christians seem to thrive and do well, while others struggle.

   1. Illustration: Some believers are like children who are victims of a disease called progeria. Children who have this disease grow old and die before they attain adulthood.

   2. Those who do well spiritually are like children who develop strong bodies because they get proper food that is available to those who take advantage of it.

   3. Those who struggle to survive spiritually are like children who are physically malnourished, even though there is healthy food available.

D. The writer of Hebrews is addressing Christian maturity in Heb. 5.

   1. Throughout this year we will follow the lessons in this chapter so we may become mature Christians.

   2. The writer of Hebrews is trying to help believers understand that Jesus is a high priest after the order of Melchizedek. If they can grasp this, they will receive great spiritual stamina. Read the scripture. (Heb. 5)

I. Lesson One—Maturity Is Not Automatic (v. 12)

A. To mature, we must do some things to help ourselves.

   1. The immaturity of the Hebrew believers is due to a failure to take advantages of opportunities that are available to them.

   2. In the same way that certain physical activities contribute to healthy physical activities, there are spiritual activities that contribute to spiritual maturity.

B. Some ways of measuring our level of maturity could include:
   1. Is my life controlled by feeling or fact?
   2. Am I self-centered or God-centered?
C. Resolve to make this a year when you practice the principles of maturity.
   1. Searching the Word regularly
   2. Praying regularly
   3. Faithfulness at all worship services

II. Lesson Two—You Can Be a Christian Infant (v. 13)

A. This chapter is written to those mentioned in Heb. 4:14 and 6:1-3.
B. It is tragic for Christians to remain infants. Illustration: Think of a tragedy that happens when a child does not grow enough to leave the nursery.

III. Lesson Three—There Are Special Pleasures for the Mature Christian (vv. 7-10)

A. The writer of Hebrews challenges believers to mature in order to know the satisfying joy of being used of God.
B. Some people live their entire lives without knowing the inner joy of being God's vessel. It is exciting to know that God has used us for His purposes.
C. The more mature we are, the greater freedom we can experience in our lives.
   1. We are not bound by the Ten Commandments. We just keep them.
   2. Things that bother immature people barely shake the fully mature.
   3. Mature believers experience the joy of reproducing themselves in the faith.

Conclusion

A. I want you to experience Christian joy that comes to mature Christians.
B. This may be the most exciting year of your life if you will follow the example of Jesus: "And the child grew and became strong; he was filled with wisdom, and the grace of God was upon him" (Luke 2:40).

A Year of Renewal

Psalm 85

Introduction

A. Our theme for this year is going to be a year of renewal.
  1. What happened last year is behind us but can be improved upon by the grace of God.
  2. Last year was a year of paradoxes. There were high times and some low times.

B. Today's scripture speaks of a similar time in Israel's history.
  1. Read Ps. 85.
  2. This psalm was written following the return of the exiles from the Babylonian Captivity.
  3. They had spent 70 years in the misery of exile.
  4. It fits the circumstances of Neh. 1, where we read that Jerusalem was only a shadow of what it should have been.

C. God is looking for some people who will enter into the spirit of renewal so that our family of believers will receive the glory that He has planned for us.
  1. We want to see verses 6 and 7 manifested in all of their potential among us.
  2. The renewal that we need will fall into two major categories.

I. A Renewal of Relationships

A. Our relationship with God
  1. This is the most critical portion of the entire plan.
  2. Our relationship with God must take top priority in our lives.
  3. Our relationship with God must be one of intensity that is the outgrowth of great love.

B. Our relationship with our families
  1. Too many homes have stale, bored relationships.
  2. There needs to be a renewal of romance between husbands and wives. Illustration: You fell in love dating. Keep on dating to sustain the love and keep it alive.

3. There needs to be a renewal of the excitement of interaction with our children.
C. Our relationships with each other
   1. Poor relationships among us will cause everyone to be a loser.
   2. We do not have to approve of everything each of us does, but neither do we have to take issue with these things. Note Matt. 7:1-3.
   3. Be sure your eyes are clear before you criticize anyone else.

II. A Renewal of Our Commitments

A. While in many ways our relationships are affected by our commitments, there is enough difference to justify a closer look.
   1. Commitments are an extension of good relationships and lead to happy associations.
   2. Illustration: Fingers are part of the extended hand. The hand and fingers are handicapped unless they are united together.
B. Our commitment to God and the church.
   1. It is difficult to enjoy the warmth of God's presence while failing to fulfill His will.
   2. What prevents me from having a daily devotional time with Him?
   3. What is more important to me than being in His house of worship?
   4. What did I buy with His tithes?
C. Our commitment to our families.
   1. What does my family need most? ME!
   2. One of the greatest weaknesses in family relationships is the lack of time spent together.
D. Our commitment to others.
   1. To let them know that I care about them.
   2. To share their joys and sorrows.

Conclusion

A. The renewal of these relationships and commitments will result in verses 10-12 being fulfilled in our midst.
B. This can be the best year any of us have ever experienced and the beginning of a great future.

SERMON OUTLINES FOR LENT AND EASTER

The Easter season is one that offers great opportunities for spiritual growth among our people. As we look at the crucifixion, burial, and resurrection of Jesus, we clearly understand that God loved us so much that He sent His only Son to pay the price for our sins. It also assures us that He will have the final say in everything that happens on the face of the earth.

In view of the fact that He has demonstrated His love for us and His power over Satan to us, the Easter season offers a marvelous opportunity to increase our faith and take courage for the future.

The opening sermon outlines on Palm Sunday, Good Friday, and Easter are all stand-alone sermon outlines that can be mixed and interspersed as needed. The next four sermon outlines are a series that will help to set the stage for the Easter season. The last three outlines are also stand-alone outlines for Easter.

Palm Sunday

Matthew 21:1-11

Introduction

   A. Jesus knew what was ahead of Him as He came into Jerusalem that day.

     1. He knew that before the Sabbath of that week, those same people would turn on Him and call for His death.

     2. He knew that false witnesses would be rounded up to tell lies about Him.

     3. He knew that before the next Sabbath, He would spend six hours suspended on a cross, where He would experience excruciating pain.

     4. He knew that many for whom He would die would hang a cross on their neck, call themselves Christians, yet like Peter would deny Him.

   B. Still, He came.

     1. No one forced Him to come.

     2. He came because He was committed to the will of His Father.

     3. Read the scripture. (Matt. 21:1-11)

I. Look at How He Came

   A. He did not come as a conqueror. His was not a mission to be won by using an army.

   B. He came to love us into the Kingdom. A one-word description of Jesus is love.

   C. While conquering generals ride into vanquished cities on horses, Jesus chose a donkey, the transportation of prophets who brought special messages from God to the people.

   D. The message Jesus carried was, "The Father genuinely loves you and has great plans for your life."

II. He Came in Joy

   A. The people were happy and rejoicing.

     1. People do not react in that manner when the leader is sorrowful and downcast.

2. Children are not attracted to unhappy people.
3. The crowd sensed no defeat in Him. They sensed His love for the Father, for them, and for life.
B. Although Jesus wept over the city as He topped the Mount of Olives because He knew the price their rejection would cost them, He knew that ultimately He would bring joy to untold millions who would accept Him.
C. The experience of the next few days would be a black hole in the history of humankind. But there would be a brilliant sunrise for the glory of God. Jesus came to do the Father's will.

III. There Was Joy in the Camp of God

A. In 1 Sam. 4 when the ark of the covenant was brought into the camp, there was such joy that the ground shook.
1. A strange thing began to happen.
2. The god of the Philistines fell on his face.
3. The Philistines sent the ark back to God's people, and that brought a celebration.
B. Jesus came into Jerusalem with great joy.
1. The enemy fought viciously and crucified Jesus.
2. It appeared that the enemy had won, but God has the final say.
C. Jesus knew that the victory belonged to His Father when He came into Jerusalem on that first Palm Sunday.
1. That is why He allowed the people to celebrate.
2. The ultimate victory belongs to the Lord.

Conclusion

A. The world in which we live is waiting for a reason to celebrate. We believers need to demonstrate the joy of the Lord to our world.
B. No one needs to wait any longer because Jesus has won the final victory.
C. Where there is victory, there is always rejoicing.

A Sermon Outline for Good Friday
The Crucifixion of Jesus

Luke 23:26-49

Introduction

A. The three greatest events in the history of the world were the birth, death, and resurrection of Jesus Christ. They are of equal importance but incomplete without each other.
   1. Our purpose today is to help us to fully realize the price Jesus paid for our sins.
   2. Read the scripture. (Luke 23:26-49)

B. Sometimes we tend to lose sight of the horror of the crucifixion of Jesus.
   1. The Cross is not just an ornament.
   2. There should never be a time when we can speak lightly of this agonizing event.

I. When I Look at the Cross, I See . . .

A. A place of suffering. It began in the Garden, but it climaxed on the Cross.
   1. The scourge—a whip made of leather with chips of bone that stripped away Jesus' flesh.
   2. The mockery, the crown of thorns.
   3. The Cross itself, intense physical pain and verbal insults.
   4. It is impossible for us to fathom the mental, physical, and spiritual sufferings of the Cross. We can only realize that it was for us—so that we might be free.

B. A place of immortal sayings.
   1. Sense Jesus' intercessory spirit as we hear Him say, "Father, forgive them, for they do not know what they are doing" (v. 34).
   2. Feel Jesus' comforting spirit as He tells the penitent thief, "Today you will be with me in paradise" (v. 43).
   3. Notice Jesus' caring love and concern for His mother. (John 19:26-27)
   4. Feel Jesus' dependence upon the Father. (Matt. 27:46)

5. Note Jesus' humanity when He expressed His thirst. (John 19:28)
6. Celebrate His victorious cry: "It is finished" (John 19:30).

C. A place of sorrow.
1. Jesus was a man with a heavy heart. (See Isa. 53.)
2. He said, "My soul is overwhelmed with sorrow" (Matt. 26:38).
3. Jesus could not be content while humanity was in bondage to sin. Sorrow for the sinful condition took Him to the Cross.

D. A place of battle.
1. Jesus fought sin in its ugliness for the souls of humankind.
2. The crowd got into the battle as they railed against Him. (Matt. 27:39-44)

E. A place of a broken heart.
1. Jesus did not die from the physical pain. He died of a broken heart.
2. There is some medical support for this position, since there was a pool of blood in the chest cavity when it was pierced with a spear.

F. A place of divine accomplishment.
1. The divine task of redemption of a sinful race was accomplished on the Cross.
2. Paul makes it clear in his statement in 1 Cor. 1:22-24.
3. Christ, the apparent Victim, was truly the Victor. And this is Calvary!

II. The Results of Calvary
A. Quote the words to the hymn "There Is a Fountain."
B. Because of Calvary, we can look God in the face, our hearts made clean, our lives restored to the beauty that God had planned in the beginning.

Conclusion
A. The Cross is no ornament.
B. It is life, love, and the assurance of sins forgiven.

The Results of the Resurrection

Matthew 28:1-8

Introduction
- A. There are some clearly established facts about Jesus.
    1. The fact that He lived when and where the Bible says is beyond question.
    2. The fact that He underwent a Roman trial and was subsequently crucified is clearly established.
    3. The fact that He somehow returned from death to life is firmly supported by as much evidence as any other event in history.
    4. Read the scripture. (Matt. 28:1-8)
- B. Look briefly at some of the evidence of the Resurrection.
    1. There are many recorded appearances of the resurrected Christ. (1 Cor. 15)
    2. Perhaps the greatest evidence of all is what happened to a band of discouraged, fearful disciples who became an irresistible force in changing their world.
    3. If Jesus had not been resurrected, why did not those who had the most to lose present His body or some tangible evidence?
- C. The answer is simple. Jesus arose! And it was that fact that sent the early believers into the world with great power.
- D. So what does that mean to you and me?

I. It Says That There Is Comfort in the Face of Sorrow
- A. The story of the two men on the road to Emmaus demonstrates this. (Luke 24)
- B. Every one of us has an Emmaus road to walk.
    1. We will walk through the valley of the shadow of death. (Ps. 23)
    2. Because of Jesus' resurrection we do not have to walk through that valley alone.
    3. The Resurrection guarantees us that love is not lost and hope is not gone.

II. The Resurrection Means That There Is Help in the Face of Frustration (John 21)
- A. Peter was a professional fisherman. He knew how to fish.

1. We read that Peter had a frustrating experience—empty nets (John 21:1-10).
   2. The resurrected Jesus came to his aid and filled his nets.
B. He still comes to help us to get through our frustrating times.
   1. We may not recognize Him at first, but we can always be sure that He is "on the shore" looking out for us.
   2. Those who listen for Him will hear His voice.
   3. Those who obey Him will experience help beyond their fondest dreams.

III. The Resurrection Means a Worthy Purpose Can Be Experienced in Our Lives (John 21)

A. Every person needs to be needed.
   1. Jesus knew that Peter needed to focus on something other than his failure.
   2. It was this opportunity that gave Peter a purpose for the rest of his life.
B. There is something for each one of us to do.
   1. No one needs to lead a meaningless life.
   2. We may feel like failures, but through His appointment we can be blessings in the lives of others.
   3. We need to love God and do what comes naturally.

IV. The Resurrection Means That We Can Have Eternal Life with Him

A. Hear the message from the apostle Paul in 1 Cor. 15.
   1. The resurrection of the dead. (vv. 12-23)
   2. What will we be like? (vv. 42-44)
   3. Because of the Resurrection—we win! (vv. 51-57)
B. This means that we will have glorified bodies. (1 Cor. 15:42-44)
C. This means we will be with our Christian loved ones forever.
D. This means we will have fellowship with Him forever. (Rev. 21:3-4)

Conclusion

A. The resurrection of Jesus means that our deepest needs have been met.
   1. Comfort in times of sorrow
   2. Help in the face of failure and frustration
B. Because Jesus lives, we have a wonderful eternity to anticipate.

The Story of Easter—Part I

1 Corinthians 15:1-19

Introduction

A. Everything we believe in revolves around Jesus and His resurrection. While for many, Easter has become little more than a comforting symbol of the immortality of the soul, it is infinitely more important than that for us.
   1. Read Paul's words in our scripture. (1 Cor. 15:1-19)
   2. Jesus is God's Son and our assurance of eternal life.
   3. In view of this, we need to give careful consideration to the story of Easter.
   4. Easter is the signal of supreme victory for the human race over sin, doubt, and defeat in our daily lives.
B. Since the Easter event is the very heart of our faith, we need to return regularly to its roots.
   1. We need to reacquaint ourselves with the main Person of the Easter story.
   2. We need to know why the story was written.
   3. We need to review once again how the story ends.
C. This initial week of this series, we will be refreshing our minds with the God-man, Jesus, around whom the Easter story revolves.

I. It Is Important to Remember That Jesus Was Very Human

A. Jesus spoke of His humanity.
   1. Matthew records 17 times when Jesus referred to himself as the "Son of Man."
   2. The root word is *anthrōpos,* which means "human being—one of the human race."
   3. Jesus is clearly identifying himself as one of us.
B. Paul spoke of the humanity of Christ. (Phil. 2:5-8) He uses the same word, *anthrōpos.*
C. Why is this important?
   1. Jesus, the main Person of the Easter story, suffered everything that we suffer as human beings.

2. This means He understands exactly how we feel in every situation.
3. The story of Easter is no shallow, symbolic myth. It is the account of a very real human being who paid a high price to succeed at the project God had given to Him—the redemption of humankind.

II. It Is Critical That We Remember That Jesus Is Also Divine

A. God the Father made sure that Peter, James, and John understood that Jesus was not just a man. (Matt. 17:1-5)
   1. Note verse 5.
   2. Moses was a great leader, but Jesus is greater. Elijah was a great prophet, but Jesus is greater.
   3. Let there be no mistake in our minds. Jesus is unique in that while He is human, He is also divine.
B. Jesus himself claimed divinity.
   1. John 14:6-10
   2. John 17:21
C. Paul wrote that Jesus is the divine Son of God. (Phil. 2:6)
D. Why is this fact such an important part of the story?
   1. If Jesus was not divine, there is no redemption for our sins.
   2. Across the centuries, on the surface many religious men have looked good. The fact remains that only Jesus offers a permanent relationship with God. (John 14:6)

III. Jesus Was God's Chosen Communicator of His Plan for Humankind

A. God said in Matt. 17:5, "Listen to him!"
B. Many voices in the world are saying good things. Only One can say, "Follow Me to the Father." (John 14:6)
C. Why is this fact so important? It clearly determines the route we must travel to experience a healthy relationship with God.

Conclusion

A. Jesus, the main Person of the Easter story, was very much a man, but He is also very much God. He is the exclusive connection between God and man.
B. In view of this, the Easter season is a wonderful time to work on our relationship with Him.

THE STORY OF EASTER—PART II
THE PLOT—REDEMPTION OF HUMANKIND

Romans 5:1-11

Introduction

A. In an attempt to make the most of this special season, we began last week to look at the story of Easter.
   1. We looked at Jesus, the main Person in this story.
   2. We considered who Jesus was and is—a very human man and a very divine man.
B. Today we will be taking a look at the plot or message of Easter. In the Easter story God's message is simple: "I love you and want to have fellowship with you."
C. In Rom. 5 Paul clearly states the heart of the story. Read verses 1-11.
D. The heart of the story is God's love vividly demonstrated on the Cross (v. 8). The Cross makes it clear we can have uninhibited fellowship with God and victory over sin. There are three great truths in this Scripture.

I. There Is Peace with God (v. 1)

A. Adam created a real problem. (v. 12)
   1. He rebelled against God. Rebellion deserves punishment.
   2. We inherited that nature, and the consequences await us. (6:23)
B. God did not abandon humankind, as He had every right to do.
   1. Rather than abandonment, He chose to reach out to us. (5:15-17)
   2. The events of Easter clearly reveal that God is reaching out to us.
C. God did not wait for us to figure out a way back to Him. (v. 10)
   1. Reconciliation means "restored to fellowship."
   2. We can have wonderful peace because of Jesus. (v. 19)

II. We Have Grace upon Which We Can Stand (v. 2*a*)

A. Not only are we reconciled and forgiven, but also we stand triumphantly.

   1. "Stand" is an active verb indicating a continuous condition of being.

   2. This is not just a passing feeling. We stand before God in peace today and will be able to remain in peace with Him tomorrow.

B. Grace is a beautiful condition in which we can live.

   1. Grace is unmerited, divine favor.

   2. In the events of Easter, God conferred dignity and honor upon us that we do not deserve.

   3. Because of Easter, we are worthy of respect now and eternally.

C. Each one of us has the opportunity to stand in the unmerited favor of God. We do not deserve it, but God is for us. Illustration: The thief on the cross did not deserve forgiveness. But God gave it to him.

III. Because of Easter, We Can Rejoice in This Present World (vv. 2*b*-3)

A. There is a dual celebration in our lives.

   1. We rejoice in the hope of heaven and eternity.

   2. We rejoice in this present world because of His forgiveness.

B. Every event in life either contributes to or detracts from the pleasure of living.

   1. By our accepting God's love, every event in life is part of our preparation for eternity.

   2. The weaknesses of our lives give opportunities for victory through God's grace. (vv. 20-21)

   3. We rejoice in this confidence. There are problems now, but because of Easter another day is coming.

Conclusion

God has prepared the message of Easter for us.

   1. Jesus, who understands every human feeling, was the sinless One.

   2. Because of His divine nature, He became our connecting link between our needs and God's endless supply of grace.

The Story of Easter—Part III

The Narrative

Introduction
A. We continue to look at the story of Easter.
1. We have looked at the Person the story revolves around. Jesus—Easter is not only history but His story.
2. He was human so that He could identify with us.
3. He is divine so that He could solve the sin problem.
4. We know why the story of Easter was written. It was written to help us realize that we are loved by God, and He wants to restore fellowship with us.
B. Today, we are going to look at the narrative of the story.
1. We will consider the story carefully. It is too important to miss any significant points.
2. We will approach this sermon outline in a different way than some of the others in that we will look at several scriptures.

I. His Entrance into the City Was Bold (Matt. 21:1-9)
A. Prior to this time, Jesus had withheld His position in the Godhead.
1. Several such occasions include:
    a. Healing of a leper (Matt. 8:4)
    b. Man with a withered hand (12:16)
    c. At the Great Confession (16:20)
2. Jesus' enemies knew that He was no ordinary person. But they did not realize His divinity.
3. One reason they were so upset was because they feared the unknown in Jesus.
B. Why did He make a public statement at this time?
1. It was time for the world to know that the Messiah had come. (Matt. 21:4-5)
2. Nature must acknowledge her Creator. (Luke 19:40)
C. Even at that time He was careful to communicate that He was not political.
1. He could have entered the city on a beautiful horse—the chosen transportation for conquering kings.
2. He chose a donkey, the transportation of God's spokesmen. (Matt. 21:5)

D. Why did Jesus come at that time?
  1. The world was finally ready.
  2. It was Passover, the time of declaring freedom for God's people. This was the most significant day on the Jewish calendar. Illustration: On July 4, 1776, those who signed the Declaration of Independence pledged their lives, their fortunes, and their sacred honor. On that day in Jerusalem, Jesus pledged His life and the treasures of heaven. The time of man's emancipation had come.

II. We Will Take a Look at the Week That Changed the World

A. It was a week of powerful experiences.
  1. The cleansing of the Temple (Matt. 21:12-13)
  2. The withering of the fig tree (vv. 18-19)
B. It was a week of great lessons.
  1. The lesson of obedience to the Father (Matt. 21:28-32)
  2. The lesson on honoring our commitment to God (vv. 33-44)
  3. A lesson on who will be comfortable in His presence (vv. 1-14)
  4. A lesson on the end of the age (Matt. 24—25)
C. It was a week of intimate experiences.
  1. The anointing at Bethany (Mark 14)
  2. Meeting with the disciples in the Upper Room (John 13)
  3. The Garden of Gethsemane prayer meeting (Matt. 26:36-45)

III. The Price Has Been Paid

A. There comes a time in every story when the plot is blatantly revealed.
  1. God had been saying, "I love you." Now He proves it at the Cross.
  2. God had said, "The price will be paid for your sins." (Isa. 53:3-5) Now the price is paid.
B. Read the description in John 19:16 ff.

Conclusion

A. The bridge has been built, and the Atonement has been completed. Those who wish to return to fellowship with the Father may do so.
B. God is saying, "Welcome home!"

THE STORY OF EASTER–PART IV
THE REST OF THE STORY

Matthew 28:1-10

Introduction

A. Newscaster Paul Harvey is famous for his phrase "And now, for the rest of the story."
   1. He is saying, "The picture is not complete until you hear what I am going to tell you."
   2. The story of Easter is not complete without today's scripture.
B. In reviewing Easter, we have considered:
   1. Who the story is about—Jesus.
   2. That the story is God's effort to tell all of us that He still loves us and is willing to forgive all of our sins.
C. Last week we looked at the narrative, the body of the story.
   1. Jesus came as a prophet, not a conquering king.
   2. He spent that last week preparing the people for what was coming.
   3. He went to the Cross to pay the price for our sins.
   4. His death was confirmed by those who crucified Him. (John 19:31-37)
D. Today, we are looking at the rest of the story. Read the scripture. (Matt. 28:1-10)

I. The Resurrection Is One of the Most Examined Events in Recorded History

A. The reason is quite obvious. Everything upon which Christianity is based is validated by the truth of this account.
B. Some simple considerations:
   1. That a man named Jesus lived when and where Jesus did is an established historical fact.
   2. That a trial and execution took place as stated in the Bible is recorded in outside accounts such as that of Josephus, the great historian. (*Josephus*, book 4, 49-50)

C. It seems that it would have been easy to verify whether or not Jesus was resurrected.
   1. Produce a body.
   2. Skeptics have had over 2,000 years to produce some evidence that Jesus was not resurrected and have failed to do so.

II. There Is No Body. HE IS RISEN!

A. He—Jesus of Nazareth—the angel clearly identifies who they were looking for. (v. 5)
B. He is alive!
   1. There are some things we anticipate with hope.
   2. There are some things that we look back upon with recognition.
   3. There are some things that are present truths. And that includes the fact of the Resurrection.
   4. The angel wanted Jesus' followers to know that He is alive and well.
   5. According to Heb. 13:8, He is still alive today.
C. He has been restored to full life.
   1. In Acts 2:24 Peter declared that while Jesus had been crucified, God had resurrected Him.
   2. The best evidence of the Resurrection is the personal experience that you and I can have with Him today.

III. How Can We Be Sure of the Resurrection?

A. That the body is gone is not debatable.
   1. This is a physically verifiable fact.
   2. Six weeks later Peter boldly declared the Resurrection in Jerusalem. (Acts 2)
B. There is irrefutable evidence of the Resurrection.
   1. Jesus was seen eight times by different witnesses. According to Paul, one appearance was witnessed by over 500 at the same time, and most of them were still living when he recorded that fact. (1 Cor. 15:6)
   2. The greatest evidence is changed lives.
      a. The lives of the disciples were transformed forever.
      b. Saul who became Paul was radically converted.
      c. Give your personal testimony.

Conclusion

A. The Lord is risen!
B. And that is the rest of the story.

Because He Lives!

Luke 24:13-35

Introduction

    A. Each year we come to the Easter season declaring the Resurrection. We do this because all of the hope of Christianity depends on this great truth. Read Paul's statement in 1 Cor. 15:13-14.

    B. This Easter we are looking at the Resurrection from a different perspective.

        1. So He lives. What does that mean to you and to me?

        2. I am assuming that you are here because you believe in the validity of the scriptural account of the Resurrection.

        3. By His resurrection, Jesus has proven that He is victorious over the worst thing that Satan can do.

        4. It is through this victory that we are able to face tomorrow with its uncertainties and potential problems.

        5. This passage demonstrates the results of the Resurrection.

        6. Read the scripture. (Luke 24:13-35)

I. The Need for Hope

    A. Look at the scene in this scripture.

        1. Two men walked sorrowfully along the road to Emmaus.

        2. They were followers of Jesus.

        3. Dreams were shattered—hope was gone. (vv. 17-21)

        4. They were full of questions without answers.

    B. The other disciples were in hiding.

        1. According to John 20:19, they had gathered behind locked doors for fear of the Jews.

        2. They appeared to be in a hopeless situation.

    C. There are many people like that in our sophisticated age.

        1. Their lives are like those described in Job 14:1-2.

        2. A look at any newspaper reveals the hopelessness that stalks the lives of many people today. Illustration: Use stories about the tragedy of suicides, drug addictions, and so on, because of hopelessness.

II. The Arrival of Hope

A. Everywhere Jesus went hope followed.
 1. The spirits of those men were lifted when they realized that Jesus was alive.
 2. People mired in sin were given a new chance. (Woman at the well—John 4)
 3. Man by the pool of Bethesda. (John 5:1-15)
 4. Lepers dying without hope. (Luke 17:11-19)

B. All that Jesus ever was He still is. (Heb. 13:8) Because He lives . . .
 1. We can face whatever situations rise in our lives.
 2. We can face a world full of war, greed, and uncertainty.
 3. We have His presence within us wherever we may be. Illustration: The pressure inside of a football is greater than all of the pressure that can be put upon it from the outside. So the power of God's strength within us can withstand whatever presses against us from without.

C. Someone has said that the tragedy of life is not death itself. It is what dies within us while we are living.
 1. Because of the Resurrection Jesus is alive and well within us.
 2. Nothing should ever fill us with sorrow to the extent that we forget the joy of our resurrected Lord living within us.

Conclusion

A. Because Jesus lives . . .
 1. A great life of inward peace and outward joy is available to all of us.
 2. Confidence and hope can be ours.

B. By His resurrection, Jesus proved that when the enemy has done his worse in our lives, God still has the final say and gives the victory.

C. Easter is not just a ritual that we go through. It is a celebration that we enjoy because He lives!

Easter—an Endless Story

1 Thessalonians 4:13-18

Introduction

A. The biography of Jesus Christ is the only one known to humankind that does not end with the death and burial of the subject.
1. The story of Jesus hastens on from chapter to chapter.
2. It is the permanence of the story of Jesus that gives us hope.
3. Read the scripture. (1 Thess. 4:13-18)

B. Most biographies of great religious leaders give an account of their birth and close with their death and resting-place.
1. Followers of Buddha can point to Buddha's resting-place in Nepal.
2. Followers of Confucius can point to his resting-place in Shantung.
3. Followers of Muhammad look to Mecca.
4. The followers of Jesus point to an empty tomb because His story never ends.

I. The Story of Jesus

A. Notice how quickly the accounts move.
1. There are a few verses about His birth and early life.
2. Much has been written about His ministry.
3. Each of the Gospels majors on the last week of Jesus' life and gives careful attention to His resurrection.

B. Jesus' death was a traumatic experience for His followers.
1. Friends begged for the body of Jesus. (Mark 15:43-45)
2. The Roman crucifiers certified His death.
3. Jesus' accusers satisfied themselves with guards at the tomb. (Matt. 27:65-66)
4. Normally, that would have been the end of the story. This is not the case with Jesus.

II. The Continuation of the Story

A. While the last chapter closed, God had more to write.
1. He did not write a notation, footnotes, or a summary.
2. Rather, it is a continuing story with no ending.

B. The story continues much like that before His death.
1. Jesus talks with His friends. (John 20:15-17, 19-29)
2. He walked with them along the road to Emmaus. (Luke 24)
3. He worked miracles for them and filled their nets with fish. (John 21:5-6)
4. He ate with them. (John 21:12-13)
5. Jesus has not changed.
C. How can this be?
1. His enemies satisfied their angry desires and wrote "Finished" to His life.
2. God the Creator had something else in mind and continues the story.
3. God has determined that death will not be the end.
4. Death may stalk our lives from the cradle to the grave. But God has reserved for himself the final victory.

III. The Story Goes On . . .
A. The apostle Paul caught the implication of the continuing story of Jesus.
1. He met Jesus on the road to Damascus, and his life was transformed.
2. He spent his life traveling the world to continue the story of Jesus.
3. In 2 Tim. 4 Paul testifies to the continuation of the story.
4. He is saying that although he has been through many things and death is looming, he is going on to a better and eternal chapter.
B. We who know Jesus as the Lord of our lives perpetuate that same story.
1. Because Jesus is alive, there is always another chapter for us.
2. Quote Paul's statement in 1 Cor. 15:20.
3. We join Paul in saying that this is not the end. The best is yet to come.

Conclusion
A. At the close of each of the obituaries of each of His children, God adds, "There will be a tomorrow."
1. This is why we can face heartache triumphantly. (2 Cor. 4:8-9)
2. This is why death does not frighten us.
B. All of us who believe in Christ have a tomorrow because Easter is an endless story.
C. Read scripture again. (1 Thess. 4:13-18)

Then Came Sunday!

John 20:1-18

Introduction
- A. Preparing an Easter sermon outline is always a challenge because we wonder what new thing can be said about Easter.
- B. The fact is that there is only one message: Jesus is alive!
- C. John took 9 of the 21 chapters in his Gospel to impress upon his readers the importance of the last week of Jesus' life.
- D. Our scripture for today involves John 20:1-18. Read the scripture.

I. The Week That Changed the World Begins in John 12:12
- A. Sunday—the day of triumphal entry.
  1. This was the day when Jesus chose to let the world know who He was.
  2. Until this time Jesus had commanded His disciples to tell no person.
  3. On that Sunday the time had come, and something had to give. According to Luke 19, it was either the people or nature itself.
- B. Monday—a day of power.
  1. We read in Mark 11 that Jesus cleared the Temple.
  2. This is what we would call going into the lions' den. It was a face-to-face confrontation with the powers of evil.
- C. Tuesday—a day of confrontation and teaching.
  1. We read about Jesus' confrontation with leaders of the Jews in Mark 11.
  2. It was a day of beautiful lessons. (John 12:20-26)
- D. Wednesday—a day of preparation.
  1. We read in Mark 13 that Jesus was preparing His disciples for the last things.
  2. Jesus was preparing himself for sacrifice. (Mark 14)
- E. Thursday—a day of tenderness.
  1. Jesus knew what was in store for His disciples. He wanted them to know how much He loved them and to give them confidence and assurance.

2. The Upper Room and the Passover meal. (Luke 22:15-20)
3. The humility of washing the disciples' feet. (John 13:4)
4. A message of hope. (John 14)
5. A promise of usefulness. (John 15)
6. A prayer for them. (John 17)

F. Gethsemane's agony brought Jesus into Friday.
1. The prayer of commitment. (Luke 22:39-46)
2. The betrayal by Judas. (Luke 22:47-48)

G. Friday—a day of intense suffering.
1. The frustration of the trials.
2. The agony of the Crucifixion.
3. The disciples were petrified with fear and went into hiding. (John 20:19)

II. Then Came Sunday!

A. The Resurrection was a total surprise to them.
1. They went to the tomb expecting to find a body. (Luke 24:1)
2. They could not comprehend the reality of the Resurrection. (Luke 24:13-24)

B. The appearance that brought assurance. (John 20:19)
1. Even doubting Thomas got help. (John 20:26)
2. For 40 days Jesus appeared to His disciples to give them confidence and assurance.
3. Jewish rulers could not dampen their confidence.
4. The Romans had the power to jail, threaten, and even kill, but they could not destroy the disciples' confidence.

C. They had Sunday, the day of resurrection, and that proved to them that God is still in control of this world.
1. When Satan and life had done their worst, God stood triumphant over everything.
2. Nothing any human could do prevented God from making Sunday the day of ultimate victory.

Conclusion

A. We, too, can have this Sunday experience in our lives.
1. Fear is removed and frustrations are solved.
2. Confidence is restored, hurts are healed, and victory is assured.

B. Sunday is here!
1. He is alive! This is the day of victory.
2. When life brings its worst, God gives His best.

LIKE MOTHER, LIKE CHILD

Hebrews 11:23 (Jochebed—Moses); Acts 12:12 (Mary—John Mark); 2 Timothy 1:5 (Eunice—Timothy)

Introduction
A. It is impossible to evaluate the influential power that a mother has on her children.
1. Many tributes have been given to this truth.
2. It is reported that Abraham Lincoln said, "All that I am I owe to my darling mother."
3. While we do not want to take the responsibility from fathers, the very nature of our society demonstrates the enormous impact of mothers on our lives.
B. There is no substitute for motherhood.
1. While others may help to care for and raise a child, a mother relates best to that child during his or her most tender and teachable years.
2. A mother is a child's best caregiver.
3. We will read the scripture as we look at three great illustrations of motherhood.

I. Jochebed, the Mother of Moses (Exod. 2:1-3)
A. Jochebed exhibited great faith in God.
1. There is no other reason that she would have risked her life to save her son. (v. 2)
2. She fully trusted Moses to the protection of God. (v. 3)
3. She instilled pride in Moses that he was one of God's people.
4. God arranged for her to be Moses' mother during his most teachable years.
B. Note Moses' response in Heb. 11:24-25.
1. His heathen environment did not influence his life choices.
2. Note verse 27. Since Moses' mother was not afraid, neither was he.

3. Note verse 29. Fear of water was no problem to him. (See Exod. 1.)

C. From his earliest days, this child was infected with faith in God by his mother. We cannot help but conclude that Moses became God's vessel to lead the Israelites to freedom because of his mother's influence.

II. Mary, the Mother of John Mark (Acts 12:12)

A. Mary created an atmosphere that had a great influence on her son, John Mark.
   1. Her home was a meeting place for the early followers of Jesus.
   2. It was normal for people of faith to be in her home.
   3. John Mark was surrounded by believers and came to great personal faith in Jesus.

B. Mary infected her son with such a faith in Jesus and love for His followers that earthly situations could not overcome that faith.
   1. Many believe that he wrote the Gospel of Mark.
   2. He accompanied Paul and Barnabas on the first missionary journey. (Acts 13:5)

C. It is still the option of mothers to infect their children with a spirit of faith. Do your children see Jesus in your daily life?

III. Eunice Had a Wonderful Influence on Her Son, Timothy (2 Tim. 1:5)

A. The godly impact on Timothy actually goes back another generation to his grandmother, Lois.
   1. The faith of Lois infected Eunice, who passed it on to Timothy.
   2. His father was probably not a Christian. But his mother's faithfulness caused him to believe in Jesus.
   3. We know more about Timothy than about Eunice.

B. His name literally means "honoring God."
   1. Timothy was Paul's closest companion for 17 years.
   2. In 1 Tim. 1:2, Paul called him "my true son in the faith."
   3. How did Timothy become such a powerful man of faith? It was his mother's influence.

Conclusion

A. Mothers are still shaping the lives of their children.

B. The raw materials to change the world are in the hands of our mothers.

"Honor . . . Thy Mother"

Ephesians 6:1-3

Introduction

A. Mothers are invaluable.
1. Some things are produced routinely and may not be worth much.
2. Other things have a lasting beauty, are reliable and durable, and have great value.
3. Motherhood is a treasure beyond description. Illustration: Good mothers are like diamonds. They are beautiful, durable, and limited in number.
4. Motherhood is what Solomon had in mind in Prov. 31:10-31.

B. Moses said, "Honor . . . your mother" (Exod. 20:12).
1. Every mother is one of a kind and has eternal value.
2. In Ephesians Paul picked up the only commandment that carries a promise.
3. Those children who have a good relationship with their parents enjoy a better quality of life than those who do not.
4. Read the scripture. (Eph. 6:1-3)

I. What Is a Mother?

A. What qualifies a woman to be called a mother?
1. A mother is not just a person who gives life.
2. Illustration: Giant sea turtles lay eggs in giving life but totally abandon their young. They are not mothers.

B. Mothering is much more than giving birth.
1. Mothering is creating an environment that causes a child to live well.
2. It means caring, feeding, loving, nurturing, protecting.
3. It means giving quality and value to the continuation of life.
4. Some have given this quality of life to children they did not bring into the world.

5. Normally we receive our sense of aesthetic values, sensitivity, tenderness, and emotional stability from our mothers. In many cases we get strength, work ethics, and physical development from our fathers.

6. While many things have changed in our world, one thing is still true. Everyone needs those qualities that only a mother can instill in each of us.

C. Mothers are very special. They are the healing arms of society. Illustration: Many children have been loved through illnesses by mothers who stayed with them in their hospital rooms.

II. How Should We Treat Our Mothers, Who Are So Important in Our Lives?

A. Paul said that we should honor them.
1. The word *honor* literally means to esteem, to value as precious.
2. It also means to pay appropriate tribute to the ones who have done such special things.

B. Some of the ways of paying tribute and showing our mother how valuable she is would include:
1. Treat her with respect. Pay attention to her opinions even if you disagree.
2. Show gratitude for the things she has done for you. Illustration: By the time you are 18 years old, she has prepared 20,000 meals and many other services for you.
3. Live a life that she can be proud of.
4. Let her know that you love her.
5. Take time for her—especially as she grows older.

Conclusion

A. Moses said (Deut. 5:16) and Paul repeats, "Honor your . . . mother . . . that it may go well with you."
1. God is pleased when we keep His commandments.
2. God is exalted when the world sees us demonstrating respect and honor for our mothers.

B. Mothers, we honor you today and pledge to honor you in the days ahead.

In Memory

Hebrews 11:32—12:3

Introduction

A. Tomorrow is Memorial Day.

    1. It is a day when we pay special tribute to our deceased loved ones.

    2. By decorating the graves of our loved ones, we are saying, "You did not live and die in vain. Your life meant something to me. You are not forgotten."

B. This is the message of Heb. 12:1-3.

    1. The 11th chapter of Hebrews is commonly called the "faith chapter." It is that, but it is also more than that.

    2. Chapter 11 contains the roles of outstanding men and women who by demonstrating their faith in God made a difference in their world.

    3. In Chapter 12 the writer is saying, "Remember these who changed their world. Go and do likewise."

    4. Read the scripture. (Heb. 11:32—12:3)

C. As we reflect upon the spiritual soldiers of the past, we will be challenged to a faith that has three important dimensions.

I. Belief in the Miraculous Intervention of God in the Affairs of Man

A. Noah is a beautiful illustration of such faith. (Heb. 11:7)

    1. He believed that God was going to do something that had never happened before.

    2. As a result of his faith, his family was saved.

B. Abraham is a powerful illustration of faith in God (Heb. 11:8-12). In Rom. 4:20, Paul wrote, "He did not waver through unbelief."

C. Do we honestly believe that God is in control of the world?

    1. Remembering the people of chapter 11, we are compelled to say, "Yes!"

    2. In the spirit of Noah defy a hostile world and save your family.

3. In the spirit of Abraham "prepare a nursery."

II. A Faith That Honors God Even in the Face of Great Obstacles

A. Again, the message of God's Word is clear.
   1. Moses' confrontation of Pharaoh (Heb. 11:27)
   2. Joshua's entrance into Canaan despite the negative feasibility report of 10 spies.
B. When was the last time you demonstrated faith in the face of a great obstacle?
   1. Who sees your faith in the face of obstacles and is compelled to believe in God?
   2. Satan tells us, "Live that way, and people will laugh at you." God says, "Live by faith, and I will put a smile on your face."

III. A Faith That Holds Believers Steady in the Face of Hostile Circumstances

A. God is especially glorified when someone pays the ultimate price. Read Heb. 11:35*b*-38*a*. By faith these people were able to face overwhelming opposition.
   1. Jesus paid the ultimate price. (Heb. 12:1-3)
   2. We are the beneficiaries of that awesome sacrifice.
B. Through the ages God exalted by the faith of those who held steady in the face of hostility and persecution.
   1. Illustration: Corrie ten Boom kept the faith in a concentration camp. As a result, millions have been inspired by her story.
   2. As we remember those who passed their faith along to us, we will be encouraged and challenged to finish the race that is set before us.

Conclusion

A. God is telling us to reflect upon the lives of those who brought the faith to us.
   1. Look up to Him for strength, courage, and guidance.
   2. Look forward to what He will do through your life.
B. There is a great cloud of witnesses who have set a wonderful example before us. And may those who follow us be inspired by our faithfulness.

Worthy of Remembering

Philippians 4:4-9

Introduction

    A. What does Memorial Day mean to you?
        1. To some it is simply a holiday.
        2. It should be a day for us to pay respect to those who have influenced our lives.

    B. There is a tendency to forget the things we should remember and to remember the things we should forget.
        1. Jesus prepared His disciples by saying, "Do this in remembrance of me" (Luke 22:19).
        2. They had many options for memories: miracles, opposition, deliverances, and so on. But Jesus wanted them to remember Him.

    C. In today's text, Paul calls for a deliberate preparation of the mind.
        1. Read the scripture. (Phil. 4:4-9)
        2. In verse 8 Paul writes, "Fix your minds" (AMP.).
        3. This calls for a deliberate act of the will.
        4. Paul is placing direct responsibility upon each one of us for what we think.
        5. What we watch, read, and feed into our minds will determine what we think about in our relaxed moments.
        6. A major part of what we think is a direct result of our priorities.
        7. Still, we can apply the truth of this passage to another area of our lives—the memories that we build.

    D. The human mind is like a computer that we program throughout our lives. The deliberate recollection of certain things determines the pattern of our lives.

I. Remember Our Spiritual Heritage

    A. We are indebted to the heroes of the faith as reiterated in Heb. 11. This is not just a Hebrew heritage. It is ours as well. Remember the heroes of the New Testament—our Lord himself and those who gave their lives for the faith, Peter, Paul, John, and others.

B. Remember our historical heritage—Martin Luther, John Hus, and many more who gave their lives for their faith.

C. Remember those of more recent history who provided so much for us—our denominational forefathers and those who founded this church in which we worship.

D. Fix your mind upon those people and pay tribute to them.

II. Remember Our Secular Heritage

A. Remember those who have paid a huge price for this great country. We owe something to everyone who has ever died fighting for America.

B. Remember those in your family who have passed the faith on to you.

   1. Some will have stronger feelings of gratitude than others.

   2. Those of us who have a godly heritage are deeply blessed.

III. Remembering Makes Life More Precious

A. As we pay tribute to the past, the present takes on a new sense of value.

   1. Illustration: A watch may be inexpensive unless it is the one my father carried.

   2. Life can seem cheap unless someone has given it special meaning.

B. The deliberate exercise of fixing our minds on those things that are worthy eliminates much of that which would trouble us.

C. In verse 9, Paul gave the Philippians a formula for a mind at peace. This formula still works today if we will practice it in our lives.

Conclusion

A. Life *is* what we make of it.

B. Ninety percent of what happens in our lives is a direct result of the priorities that we set.

C. As Paul instructed the Philippians, let us fix our minds on those things that are worthy of remembering.

A Good Picture of God

Psalm 103:1-14

Introduction
 A. All of us have wondered what God is like.
  1. It is interesting to study the pictures of God that children have drawn.
  2. A child is reported to have said, "Jesus is the best picture God ever took."
  3. Because we are physical beings, we have the need to relate God to a physical concept.
 B. Jesus understood this need and helped us by using the term "Father."
  1. In Luke 2:49 we read Jesus' first recorded words, "Didn't you know I had to be in my Father's house?"
  2. In Luke 23:46 we read Jesus' last words before He died, "Father, into your hands I commit my spirit."
  3. After the Resurrection, in John 20:17, Jesus said, "I am returning to my Father and your Father, to my God and your God."
  4. He is clearly calling attention to God as a "Father."
 C. In Ps. 103, David describes God's wonderful, providential care. He rises to the peak moment by describing God as a Father.
 D. Read the scripture. (Ps. 103:1-14)

I. Why Did Jesus Use the Term "Father" to Describe God?
 A. There are many other names that could be used.
  1. Shepherd—but not everyone could identify with this.
  2. Brother—but not everyone has a brother.
  3. Pastor—but not everyone could understand this.
  4. Mother—but in the biblical model, the father is the head of the household.
  5. "Father" is the strongest term with which we can all identify.

6. The qualities of a good father are those that make God so meaningful to us.

B. David lists some of these qualities in this psalm.
   1. We read in verse 2, "Forgot not all his benefits." A good earthly father provides for every area in the lives of his children.
   2. In verse 3 we read that the Father works to correct the weaknesses in our lives.
   3. In verse 4 life is raised to its highest possibility.
   4. In verse 5 the psalmist emphasizes that the Father enables us to find renewal. (See Isa. 40:31 for more details.)
   5. In verses 8-10 we read that the Father is merciful and kind.

C. The things that make a man a good father are all found in God. If we were designing a perfect father, these are the qualities we would desire.

II. The Most Beautiful Part of David's Description Is Found in Verse 13

A. In the same way that a father is tender and sympathetic, so is God.

B. Fathers feel what their children feel. Illustration: The father of a young lady bought a pony for her because she loved horses, even though he was not interested in them. He wanted to do everything in his power to show that he cared about what was important to his daughter.

C. Fathers help their children make the most of their dreams.
   1. Illustration: Mickey Mantle was one of the greatest baseball players of all time. His father spent every day after work practicing with him.
   2. Give your personal testimony of how God has blessed your life.

Conclusion

A. In Ps. 103 David paints a beautiful picture of God, our Heavenly Father, with whom everyone can relate.

B. The qualities of God that we find in this psalm are the ones that we would hope to have in our earthly father.

C. All earthly fathers should focus on letting these qualities become a part of their lives.

Men in the Will of God

Ezekiel 22:30-31

Introduction

    A. The text comes from God's desire to turn Israel from her sinful ways to what He had planned for them.

        1. God had a beautiful plan for His people, but they kept straying. (vv. 6-12)

        2. Still, God kept on reaching out to them.

        3. The text declares that God has sought for a man to be His vehicle to deliver His people.

        4. Read the scripture. (Ezek. 22:30-31)

    B. The call goes out today. Is there a man I can use today to bring the people into the beautiful experience I have in mind?

        1. This is true of natures, churches, and families.

        2. God is saying, "I need men who care enough to let Me work through them."

    C. For some mysterious reason, God has always chosen to work through people.

I. God Used Men in the Old Testament

    A. He used Adam to begin the human race. (Gen. 1:28)

    B. God used Noah to repopulate the earth after the Flood. (Gen. 6—9)

    C. He used Moses to deliver the people. (Exod. 3 ff.)

    D. He used many others.

        1. Elijah—to declare His power. (1 Kings 18)

        2. Isaiah—to declare His holiness. (Isa. 6)

    E. The Old Testament is rich with experiences that clearly demonstrate what happened when God found a man to stand in the gap.

II. God Used Men in the New Testament

    A. God continued to work through men to provide the beautiful life He had in mind.

    B. Joseph, a carpenter, was chosen to be Jesus' earthly father. Evidence indicates that there was special relationship between Jesus and Joseph.

C. A group of fishermen were selected to spread the Good News.
   1. They were not academically qualified. Yet, Jesus used them.
   2. They were entrusted with the greatest story ever told.
D. Paul, a teacher of religion, became God's greatest missionary.
   1. Paul had many options because of his training.
   2. God used him to "make up the hedge" and to provide the whole world with the good news of Jesus.
E. There are many more.
   1. Luke—the physician and companion of Paul.
   2. Matthew—the tax collector and keeper of the genealogy of Jesus.
   3. Aquila—a tentmaker who was Paul's friend.
F. Every time God found an available man, He used him.

III. God Continues to Use Men
A. God used men throughout the pages of history.
   1. Martin Luther—to reform His church
   2. John Wesley—to birth a great holiness movement
   3. Dwight L. Moody—to start a revival
B. God looks for men today who will stand in the gap.
   1. He looks for men from every profession who will be available for the work of the Kingdom.
   2. He seeks men who will demonstrate to their families the model for all families.
   3. It is critical that God will be able to find men today who will step into the gap and be used by Him.
C. In our text, the comment "but I found none" is a statement of disaster.
   1. Note verse 31.
   2. This could have been avoided if God had found a man.

Conclusion
A. God looks for men today.
   1. Where He finds them, there is a beautiful life.
   2. Where He does not find them, there is heartache and ruin.
B. I am available. Are you?

FIVE GREAT FREEDOMS

Romans 8

Introduction
    A. There are many types of freedoms that we may enjoy today.
       1. Political, financial, from illness, and from problems.
       2. No one experiences all of these freedoms.
    B. In Rom. 8, Paul addresses five great freedoms available to everyone.
       1. Read the scripture: Rom. 8:1-2, 12-18, 22-28, 35-39.
       2. These freedoms are given to those not only who turn their sins over to Jesus but also who surrender control of their lives to Him.

I. Freedom from Fear of Spiritual Failure (vv. 1-2)
    A. Paul emphasizes the fact that we can experience freedom from the guilt that comes as a result of spiritual failure.
    B. The key to living with this freedom is found in Rom. 8:1 (AMP.): "Who live [and] walk not after the dictates of the flesh, but after the dictates of the Spirit."
       1. Living after the flesh submits one to slavery to the appetites.
       2. Living in the Spirit means freedom from the tyranny of the flesh.

II. Freedom from the Fear of God (vv. 12-15)
    A. When a person is filled with the Spirit, he or she is set free from fear of our Heavenly Father. *"Abba,* Father" is a term that speaks of a tender, loving relationship. How can one fear a Father for whom he or she has warm feelings?
    B. What is your attitude toward God?
       1. Is He awesome and frightening?
       2. Or is He warm and loving?

III. There Is Freedom in Prayer (vv. 26-27)
    A. Prayer is a real problem for some people.
       1. They are afraid that they will not get the words right.

2. We do not need to worry about the words. God hears what we are trying to say.
    B. The Spirit intercedes for us so that we do not need to worry about getting it right. Note verse 26 in the *Amplified Bible*: "So too the [Holy] Spirit comes to our aid *and* bears us up in our weakness; for we do not know what prayer to offer *nor* how to offer it worthily as we ought, but the Spirit Himself goes to meet our supplication and pleads in our behalf with unspeakable yearnings and groanings too deep for utterance."
    C. This freedom in prayer enables us to have a deeper relationship with God.

IV. Freedom from Fear of Circumstances (v. 28)
    A. The possibilities of life can be terrifying.
        1. Life is not an easy journey.
        2. In John 16:33 Jesus said, "In this world you will have trouble. But take heart! I have overcome the world."
    B. Spirit-filled people have a special consolation.
        1. We know that God has the final say in every situation.
        2. Moffatt translates this: "We know also that those who love God, those who have been called in terms of his purpose, have his aid and interest in everything."
        3. This frees us from fear of those things that are beyond our control.

V. Freedom from Fear of Falling (vv. 35-39)
    A. This final freedom assures of fellowship with our Heavenly Father. Some Christians live in a petrified state, afraid they will do something wrong. God has a better plan.
    B. The Spirit-filled Christian lives in absolute confidence.
        1. This liberty allows us to let ourselves go in Him.
        2. Like Paul, we face life with the assurance he expresses in Phil. 4:13.

Conclusion
    A. This chapter begins with no condemnation and ends with no separation.
    B. These great freedoms belong to all of those who do not live according to the physical things of life but after the Spirit of God.

ONE NATION, UNDER GOD

Introduction

   A. What is it that makes America the greatest nation on earth?
1. Many countries have longer historical roots.
2. There are nations with much larger geographical areas.
3. There are nations with much larger populations.

   B. Something special makes the United States the greatest nation.
1. It has a special quality that we want to address today.
2. It is easy to be blinded by our critics and the cynics who constantly emphasize our nation's weaknesses.
3. We lose sight of "America the Beautiful" when we just see the problems.
4. We should lift our heads and hearts high because we are citizens of this great nation.

I. What Is It That Makes America Great?

   A. Is it her vast resources?
1. You name it—and we have it.
   a. Minerals—the precious and the practical of which we have a 500-year supply.
   b. Land—while there are crowded corridors, there are vast, open plains.
   c. Forests—Although they may not be inexhaustible, if we manage them well, they are abundantly adequate.
2. If we learn to practice the proper stewardship of our nation's resources, they will never fail us.
3. Still, there is something greater.

   B. Perhaps our greatness is found in our philosophy of freedom.
1. Where else can we find a nation whose people can speak their minds in criticism of their government?
2. There is a freedom in America that is unequaled anywhere else in the world.
3. This freedom cost our forefathers a great price and will cost us something to maintain it.

   C. In searching for the source of our greatness, we need to remember our ingenuity.

1. We have a way of solving problems.
2. Think of the health issues that we have solved.
3. Consider the travel and communication problems that we have solved.

D. Still, none of these attributes are the true source of our greatness.

II. In God We Trust

A. Our strength and greatness stem from something inexhaustible and incorruptible—our faith in God.
1. We are a nation founded on faith in God.
2. Take note of the Declaration of Independence.
3. Abraham Lincoln is quoted as having said in his first inaugural address: "We are almost a chosen nation."

B. There have always been those who would turn us aside from those roots.

There is a continuous effort to try to sever us from our faith in God. Illustration: Use a recent story of a court-ordered separation of church and state.

C. Periodically, someone rises up to bring us back to our roots.
1. In 1861 Salmon P. Chase, secretary of the treasury, wrote to the director of the U.S. Mint, "No nation can be strong except in the strength of God or safe except in His defense. The trust of our people in God should be declared on our national coins." Then he instructed the director to prepare a motto for our currency. On April 22, 1864, an act was passed authorizing that the words "In God we trust" be inscribed on our coins.
2. In 1954 Congress acted to place the words "under God" in the Pledge of Allegiance.
3. The spiritual heritage of America is the taproot of our way of life.

D. We are nation of great variety. But we are unified.
1. Many denominations—but one faith.
2. Many practices and ceremonies—but one faith.
3. Denominations rise and fall. But the faith remains. And so does America.

Conclusion

A. What is that makes America the greatest nation on earth? It is not our resources, not our philosophy of freedom, not our ingenuity.

B. We are the greatest nation on earth because we are "one nation, under God."

THE SECOND REFORMATION

Romans 3:21-31

Introduction

    A. On October 31, 1517, the Protestant Reformation began.
1. Martin Luther nailed 95 theses to the door of the Wittenberg Church in Germany.
2. This one man determined to do everything in his power to change the course of his world.
3. He had a position of respect in the church but was challenged in his heart to make a difference in his world.
4. The result brought difficult days but ultimately success as it signaled the birth of the Protestant Church.

    B. We need a Second Reformation today. We need a reformation of the moral principles of this nation. Illustration: A look at the daily newspaper or evening news makes this blatantly clear.

    C. Luther's belief was the result of his reading the Book of Romans. Today, we will look at one chapter of that book that changed the world. Read the scripture. (Rom. 3:21-31)

I. Look at the Principles of Protestantism

    A. We believe that the just shall live by faith.
1. Luther's problem was the Catholic teaching of penance and performance of indulgences for sin.
2. He believed that there was something better—faith in God's grace. The truth that he found in verses 21-24 is simply that faith is the key.

    B. We believe that the Word of God is our authority.
1. It is the standard for judging all truth.
2. Luther focused on the truth of God's Word.
3. He determined that tradition has value only insofar as it is based on Scripture.

    C. We believe that laypeople should participate in the worship experience. Congregational singing is the result of the Reformation. Christianity is not a two-platoon system. Everyone can participate.

D. We believe in the priesthood of believers. The holiness of God made Him appear to be unapproachable, and the Catholic Church had taken advantage of this. By Jesus' death on the Cross, He opened the holy of holies to everyone.

E. As Protestants we worship God with our hearts as well as our hands. The heart and soul find comfort and guidance in the Word. Since God has become the King of our hearts, we can go directly to Him. Luther gave rise to "heartfelt religion."

II. The Principles of the New Reformation

A. All of those ascribed to Luther and more apply.
   1. We add an emphasis on the validity of the new birth. (John 3:1-15)
   2. We add an emphasis on the infilling of the Holy Spirit. (Acts 1:8)

B. We would emphasize the need for high moral standards in humankind.
   1. We were not created to live by animal instincts.
   2. The seventh of the Ten Commandments still has a valid claim on our lives. Its abuse is the source of many of today's problems.

C. Today's problems are the result of a failure to live by the principles of the Word.
   1. Our situation will not improve until we return to clear biblical standards.
   2. Rom. 3:22-24 is the foundation for the New Reformation.

D. There is no doubt that there is a need for a New Reformation. The question is, Are we ready to take a stand for righteousness in our day?

Conclusion

A. When Luther was on trial for his faith, he is reported to have said, "Here I stand. I cannot do otherwise. God help me."

B. The reformation we desperately need today will come from people who have similar courage.

Here We Stand

Hebrews 13:1-14

Introduction
- A. We live in a world that is filled with turmoil and change.
  1. Science is continually making new discoveries that change our lives. Take note of the changes in medicine, travel, and communication.
  2. Standards of conduct are under constant attack.
  3. The Church in general has compromised what had been strong principles on the deity of Christ and the morality of humankind.
- B. As a result of these changes many people are confused about what they believe.
  1. The psychological nature of human beings demands a point of reference.
  2. Illustration: The permanent placement of stars and planets enable us to travel safely in space.
- C. In our spiritual lives there are some fixed points of reference to guide us on the journey of life.
- D. Read the scripture. (Heb. 13:1-14)

I. Martin Luther Was a Stable Influence in His Day
- A. The Protestant Reformation was a rebellion against uncertainty.
  1. The Catholic Church was filled with many inconsistencies.
  2. The selling of indulgences gave people permission to go on sinning, since they could buy forgiveness.
  3. While reading Rom. 3:22, Luther was awakened to the truth: "Righteousness from God comes through faith in Jesus Christ." This awakening led Martin Luther to become a force that changed his world.
- B. Luther was consistent in his stand and became a positive force in his world.
  1. In the midst of overwhelming pressure to compromise, Luther stood fast.

2. During Luther's testimony before the Diet of Worms he declared, "Here I stand. I cannot do otherwise. God help me."
3. Luther's hymn "A Mighty Fortress Is Our God" speaks of assurance.

II. Our Church Has a Stable Position to Offer

A. In a day of religious uncertainty, it is well to know what we truly believe.
   1. Our positions are strong and inflexible.
   2. We are not narrow and exclusive in our spiritual confidence. We do believe that we have an appointed destiny in this world.
   3. We are what we are because of what we believe.
B. These truths are not subject to arbitration. They are firm and steadfast, and a person can build an eternal life based on them.
C. We believe that God created the heavens and the earth. There is no other reasonable, sensible alternative.
D. We believe that the Bible is the inspired Word of God. As fantastic as it seems, all of it is easily proven to be true if we accept the reality of God.
E. We believe in the deity of Jesus Christ. He is the Son of God and Savior of the world.
F. We believe that there is a remedy for sin. The love of God forgives us, and the power of God transforms our lives.
G. We believe in being filled with the Holy Spirit. It is this filling that enables us to live believable lives daily.

Conclusion

A. We stand firm in the faith that there is a triumphant life available for all who take a clear stand for their faith.
   1. We firmly declare that Jesus can solve the sin problems in life and that the Holy Spirit can make us victorious.
   2. We believe that it is essential that Christians become firmly established in their hearts, minds, and lives.
   3. This faith becomes a point of reference in a topsy-turvy world.
B. As we take our stand, we will not be understood, and we may face opposition. Yet, like Martin Luther, for the good of the world and the Kingdom—Here We Stand!

Sermon Outlines for Thanksgiving
An Attitude of Gratitude

Psalm 107:1-16

Introduction

A. Gratitude is an attitude of the soul.
   1. To be genuine, gratitude must come from within.
   2. Those who experience this condition have fulfillment rather than the constant dissatisfaction of wanting more.
   3. This lifestyle is something that cannot be forced. It is voluntary, optional, and indicative of a person's true nature.

B. Gratitude lifts life to a new level.
   1. Those who learn to appreciate kindness, blessings, and the things and health that they do have soon come to experience a more positive lifestyle than others.
   2. Those who live positively enjoy life more than those who live negatively.

C. David demonstrates the attitude of gratitude. Look at Pss. 100 and 103. Yet David had his share of problems.

D. David was not the only one who found a reason for praise. Our scripture for today was sung at the dedication of the Second Temple in 516 B.C. by the exiles who had returned from Babylon. Note their spirit in returning from a time of deep distress to freedom and joy. Read the scripture. (Ps. 107:1-16)

E. Today, we will enjoy life more if we develop this same attitude of gratitude.

I. The Attitude of Gratitude Toward Those Around Us

A. We all have someone who has had a positive impact on our lives.
   1. It is easy to recall the bad things that have been said and done to us.
   2. It is far better to remember the good things that have been said and done to us. This creates a good feeling in our hearts.

B. Every person that I have ever met has made a contribution to my life.
   1. My friends are an encouragement to me.
   2. My critics made me a better person.
C. All of us live in one of four modes.
   1. Getting—always taking, receiving from others.
   2. Giving—always doing something for others, never letting anyone help us.
   3. Graciously giving when able, yet getting when needed.
   4. Being alone—no love or fellowship with others.
D. What kind of an attitude do you have toward those around you? Your answer will determine much of your pleasure or lack of joy in your life.

II. The Attitude of Gratitude Toward God
A. The psalmist tells us that God has something special for His people.
   1. In verses 5-9 we read that God cares for our physical needs.
   2. In verses 10 and 14 we read that God cares for our emotional needs.
   3. In verse 13 we read that God comforts us in times of distress.
   4. In verse 14 we read that God frees us from bondage.
   5. In appreciation for God's blessings, the psalmist calls for thanksgiving.
B. God has done many of the same things for all of us. Some of those things that we take for granted are great blessings that we would not want to lose. Illustration: The five senses and the air that we breathe mean so much to us.
C. How can we show our gratitude to God?
   1. By expressing words of thanksgiving as the psalmist has done. (vv. 1-2)
   2. By acts of service toward God and others.
   3. By simply living with an attitude of gratitude in our lives.

Conclusion
When we realize all God has done for us, we will want to express our thanksgiving. Sing the Doxology.

An Exercise Worth Repeating

Psalm 103

Introduction

A. There has been a dramatic rise in exercising among Americans.
   1. Illustration: List various kinds of activities that people are doing.
   2. We realize that physical exercise is good for our health.
      a. Many are jogging.
      b. Some are doing weight training.
      c. Others are involved in aerobics.
B. There is another area of our lives in which we need to have regular exercise. That is in expressing our appreciation.
   1. There is no doubt that vigorously indulging in saying thanks will enhance our spiritual, physical, and emotional well-being.
   2. As we read today's scripture, we can see that David calls for this exercise of appreciation.
   3. Read the scripture. (Ps. 103)
C. In this psalm David is pushing himself in the exercise of thanksgiving to God.
   1. Could this be the reason he had such a healthy relationship with God?
   2. Could this be why he is described in Acts 13:22 as "a man after [God's] own heart"?
   3. Could this explain the fact that there is a genuine note of pleasure in his life that made him the psalm singer of Israel?
D. We want to begin today to indulge in this exercise with David.

I. We Will Warm Up by Calling to Mind Benefits for Which We Are Thankful

A. Our heritage—in His kindness, God has granted us the heritage of a Christian atmosphere in which we can live.
   1. It is more than a religion. Our Christian heritage is a way of life that brings out the best in each one of us.

2. Alex Haley's book *Roots* made him a wealthy man. Our roots make us children of the King.
B. Our home—many of us were privileged to be reared in Christian homes.
   1. This is a blessing that we do not dare to overlook.
   2. Being brought up in a Christian home is one of the greatest blessings that we can receive and pass on to our children.
C. Our health—we thank God for the health that He has given to us.
   1. While it is true that some of us have illnesses, we do not have to look far to find someone who would change places with us. Illustration: Fanny Crosby, Helen Keller, and Joni Eareckson Tada have all learned to live with physical problems.
   2. We can enjoy what we have if we stay away from focusing on what is wrong.
D. Our happiness—most of us have much more joy than we realize.
   1. Happiness is the deep inner sensation of joy.
   2. It is not based on anything physical, mental, or emotional.
   3. Happiness is not controlled by external circumstances but by internal conditions.
E. Our hope—people without hope are miserable and to be pitied.
   1. As believers we praise God because He has given us a "living hope" (1 Pet. 1:3).
   2. Paul wrote in Rom. 12:12 that we are to "be joyful in hope, patient in affliction, faithful in prayer."
   3. We have hope in spite of any situation in which we find ourselves.
   4. We can be assured that God has already given the victory to someone else who has gone through a similar trial.

II. With These Blessings in Our Lives There Are Exercises to Be Performed

A. There are some options to be rejected.
   1. The assumption that the good things in my life are my own doing.

2. The feeling that I deserve these blessings because I am so special.
3. The intention to take time in the future to express appreciation.
4. The token act of just doing something so that I am aware of God's blessings.

B. The option I choose.
1. Like the woman in Mark 14:3, I will give a lavish expression of gratitude to God.
2. Her act was one of total commitment.
3. She wanted Jesus to know how pleased and grateful she was.

Conclusion

A. Today we want to do as David expressed in verses 1 and 2 as we call our souls to strong exercise of thanksgiving to God for all of His benefits to us.

B. This exercise of thanksgiving will add a great dimension to the quality of our lives.

C. We begin our exercise routine by singing the Doxology.

God's Great Grace

John 1:1-18

Introduction
- A. It is Thanksgiving season. Let's take a good look at God's goodness to us.
  1. He has blessed our lives beyond anything we could have ever deserved.
  2. Why has He blessed us, and what is our greatest praise to Him?
- B. Our passage ends by emphasizing God's great grace and continuous blessings.
- C. Read the scripture. (John 1:1-18)

I. We Are Thankful for His Saving Grace
- A. God's grace goes deeper than our ugliest sins. Illustration: It was this grace that changed the lives of Mary Magdalene, the woman at the well, Zacchaeus, and countless others.
- B. It is this amazing grace that continues to radically change lives today. Illustration: Share your personal testimony.

II. We Are Thankful for His Keeping Grace
- A. Jude, believed to be Jesus' brother, emphasizes this in verse 24. It is a wonderful thing to be able to live without fear of failure.
- B. Paul points to this same victorious life.
  1. In Rom. 5:19-21 he describes the redeeming grace of God.
  2. In Rom. 6 he declares our freedom from the tyranny of sin.
- C. We do not have to go through life being shoved around by sin.
  1. While we do not live perfect lives, neither do we need to live defeated lives. God's plan for His people is that they live victoriously.
  2. In 1 John 2:1 we read that we can have confidence in living victoriously.

3. Jesus said that He came so that we could live lives that overflow. (John 10:10)

   D. We must be grateful that we do not have to go through life being defeated by those things for which Jesus died. Illustration: In the 1992 Olympics a marathon runner came into the arena long after the others had finished. Exhausted, he fell, struggling to finish. A man suddenly appeared to help him across the finish line. He looked up into the face of his father. Our Father gets under our struggling lives so that we can finish the race.

III. We Can Be Thankful for Comforting Grace

   A. Jesus' love compels Him to be with brokenhearted people. Illustration: Jesus' journey in John 11 was made because He felt great compassion. Although it was 40 miles uphill through the desert, He came because Mary and Martha needed Him.

   B. Jesus has walked with all of us through some very uncomfortable moments.
   1. For some of us it has been the valley of the shadow of death (Ps. 23:4).
   2. For others it has been through different kinds of difficulties: health crises, family crises, financial crises.
   3. The comforting grace of our Lord has been with us.

IV. We Are Thankful for His Grace That Provides Us with a Future

   A. Paul wrote about this to the church at Thessalonica. (1 Thess. 4:13-18) This assures us that regardless of what is going on in our lives, something good is just ahead.

   B. We can be confident that God has a hope and a future for us. (Jer. 29:11) He has better plans for us than we have for ourselves.

Conclusion

   A. When we count our blessings this Thanksgiving, we will all be grateful for our health, our freedom to live in the U.S.A., our family, and our church.

   B. But the greatest blessing of all is God's grace.
   1. It is greater than our failures.
   2. It is greater than my needs.
   3. It is so great that it provides a future.

A Sermon Outline for Communion
This Cup

Luke 22:39-53

Introduction

  A. Jesus spent the last evening of His life with His disciples celebrating the Passover and preparing them for the coming events.
    1. He planted seeds of confidence. (John 14)
    2. He promised a useful life. (John 15)
    3. He encouraged them to live positively. (John 16)
    4. He prayed for them. (John 17)

  B. In Luke 22 Jesus is in the garden preparing himself for the hours just ahead.
    1. He came to talk to His Father.
    2. The most important opportunity in our lives is available as a result.
    3. Read the scripture. (Luke 22:39-53)

  C. Look at the events in the garden.
    1. Jesus' agony of the soul. (v. 44)
    2. His earnest prayer alone. (v. 45)
    3. The betrayal of an intimate friend. (v. 47)

  D. The confirmation of His commitment is found in verse 42. What is this cup that is the focal point of His prayer and agony?

I. For You and Me, the Cup Contained Three Important Blessings

  A. The cup contained forgiveness for every sin.
    1. Jesus demonstrated His desire to forgive sin while He was on the Cross—the thief.
    2. The promise of 1 John 1:9 grew out of the events of the Cross.
    3. Paul refers to the Cross in Rom. 5:8.
    4. Because of the Cross we can sing the great hymn "There Is a Fountain."

B. The cup contained freedom from the domination of sin.
   1. Paul speaks to this in Rom. 6:14 and 22.
   2. There is a beautiful picture in the Old Testament of what was happening. (Jer. 52:31-34)
C. The cup gives us a future in the presence of the Father.
   1. In John 14 Jesus talks about our future with Him.
   2. In Rev. 7 we are told who will be with us.

II. For Jesus, the Cup Contained Great Agony

A. The mockery of a trial.
   1. They looked for false witnesses. (Mark 14:55 ff.)
   2. The entire trial was illegal.
B. A scourging that was inhuman.
   1. The Romans were masters at abusing the bodies of their prisoners. (Mark 15:15)
   2. They continued to torture Jesus. (Mark 15:16-20)
C. A death so ugly that nature could not watch.
D. These events do not represent the cup to which He was referring in verse 42.
   1. Matthew describes this cup in 27:46.
   2. The cup meant the separation from the Father for the first time.
   3. When Jesus took our sins upon himself, the Father turned away.
   4. Jesus died alone because it was the only way to solve the sin problem.

Conclusion

A. We will receive the cup and bread because of this event.
B. Jesus paid the ultimate price to provide us with:
   1. A cup of forgiveness
   2. A cup of freedom
   3. A cup of a future in the presence of the Father
C. Sing the hymn "When I Survey the Wondrous Cross."

Nahum 1:7

Introduction

A. Our attitude toward God will determine the degree of darkness or light that we experience as we walk through the valley of the shadow of death.

B. It is normal to feel grief at the loss of someone dear to us.

    1. I am here to tell you that help is available for times like this.

    2. The writer of Ecclesiastes tells us that there is a time for everything in chapter 3: "There is a time for everything, and a season for every activity under heaven: a time to be born and a time to die, a time to plant and a time to uproot, a time to kill and a time to heal, a time to tear down and a time to build, a time to weep and a time to laugh, a time to mourn and a time to dance" (vv. 1-4).

    3. It is obvious that he recognizes the hurts of life. But he is pointing out that help is available.

C. This help comes from God whom Nahum describes as being good.

D. Read the scripture. (Nahum 1:7)

I. The Lord Is Good

A. We see the goodness of God in the world He created.

    1. Following the creation, we read in Gen. 1:31: "And God saw all that he had made and it was very good."

    2. Words are not adequate to describe the beauty of the world He made. Illustration: Look at the beautiful flowers that He created to be available during times of sorrow to bring comfort to a grieving family.

B. We know the goodness of God through His Word.

    1. David writes in Ps. 34:8, "Taste and see that the LORD is good; blessed is the man who takes refuge in him."

    2. In Ps. 107:1 we read, "Give thanks to the LORD, for he is good; his love endures forever." Four times in that psalm he writes, "Let them give thanks to the LORD for his unfailing love and his wonderful deeds for men."

C. We know that God is good because of the pains to which He went to bring about the redemption of humanity.
   1. It was the goodness of God that sent His Son to pay the price for our sins.
   2. Quote John 3:16.
   3. God has tasted the sorrow that we feel as we are gathered here today. He does not have to feel our sorrow, but because He is good, He does.

II. This Good God Is Our Stronghold in Times of Trouble

A. Humankind has found this to be true in every situation of life.
   1. It is comforting to know that this good God invites us to come to Him in our hour of need.
   2. In Matt. 11:28 Jesus offered the invitation for times like this.
B. God does not remove the difficulties and sorrows from our pathway, but He does provide the strength to face them.
   1. In Ps. 46:1 we read, "God is our refuge and strength, an ever-present help in trouble."
   2. In Ps. 121 we read, "I lift up my eyes to the hills—where does my help come from? My help comes from the Lord, the Maker of heaven and earth."
   3. It is amazing what we can survive when we look to the Lord for help.

III. This Good, Strong God Knows Those Who Trust Him

A. There are some blessings that come to all of us. We read in Matt. 5:45 that Jesus points to the Father, who "causes his sun to rise on the evil and the good, and sends rain on the righteous and the unrighteous."
B. Help for the great needs of life is reserved for those who trust Him.
   1. I urge you to come to Him now and realize His strength in this hour of need.
   2. Illustration: As we journey across the country, we find rest areas for weary travelers. They are only helpful to those who use them. It is the same with the promises of God.

Conclusion

The good God that Nahum offered waits for you to look to Him today.

Death Has No Sting

1 Corinthians 15:50-57

Introduction

A. For the loved ones of the deceased, the experience of death is the most difficult time imaginable.
   1. Inevitably, we must face the unanswered questions. They are: "Why?" "Could anything have prevented this?" and so on.
   2. There is a sudden emptiness within that tears at our emotions.

B. It is to you whose hearts are so heavy today that I offer the assurances of God's Word.
   1. Read the scripture. (1 Cor. 15:50-57)
   2. Paul is telling us that there is victory in the face of death.
   3. Paul is telling us that comfort is available in the face of death to bring healing to shattered emotions.
   4. Paul is writing that there is strength in the face of death for the weakness that we feel, since we could not prevent it.

C. Paul writes that death has no sting, because through the power and death of Jesus, He took it away. While death is never pleasant, because of Jesus' death we turn it into the vehicle that carries us from the world of the temporal to the world of the eternal.

D. How does Jesus take away the sting of death?

I. Jesus Is a Caring Savior

A. The Bible continuously describes Him as caring deeply for people.
   1. Isaiah had promised this in Isa. 53.
   2. We read throughout the Gospels about how Jesus constantly cares for the hurting.
   3. There are many instances of how Jesus cared for the mourners on days like this.
      a. In John 11 Jesus comforted Mary and Martha.
      b. In Luke 7 Jesus felt the sorrow of a poor widow.

       4. The most graphic picture of Jesus' caring is shown on the night before His death when He comforted His disciples in John 14.

  B. Jesus has not changed. (Heb. 13:8)
     1. He cares about our broken hearts today.
     2. Jesus did not give simple, shallow answers to the problem of dying.
     3. He came to help us walk through the valley of the shadow of death.

II. He Is an Understanding Friend

  A. Jesus brings more than sympathy.
     1. He brings hope into what happens beyond the grave. (John 14)
     2. He does not answer all of the questions but assures us of a great eternity.

  B. At this moment you should not try to understand your loved one's death.
     1. In time the curtain will be pulled back, and you will see beyond the mystery of this moment.
     2. Be assured that Jesus understands your feelings and confusion in your loss.

III. Jesus Asks You to Trust Him

  A. In the Sermon on the Mount Jesus spoke of asking and receiving. In Matt. 7:11 He states, "If you, then, though you are evil, know how to give good gifts to your children, how much more will your Father in heaven give good gifts to those who ask him!"

  B. In the garden, at a most difficult moment in His life, Jesus trusted His Father.

  C. Today, Jesus is asking you in this difficult moment to trust Him. Remember John 14:1, where He said, "Do not let your hearts be troubled. Trust in God; trust also in me."

Conclusion

  A. As we remember Jesus' care and understanding, we can trust Him fully.

  B. When we trust Him, totally trust Him, then we know, as Paul told us, that death has no sting.